Above the Birch Line

Above the Birch Line

Poems

Pia Taavila-Borsheim

Gallaudet University Press
Washington, DC

Gallaudet University Press
gupress.gallaudet.edu

Gallaudet University Press is located on
the traditional territories of Nacotchtank and Piscataway.

ISBN 978-1-944838-89-8 (paperback)
ISBN 978-1-944838-90-4 (ebook)

Library of Congress Cataloging-in-Publication Data

Names: Taavila, Pia, author.
Title: Above the birch line : poems / Pia Taavila-Borsheim.
Description: Washington, DC : Gallaudet University Press, 2021. | Summary: "This poetry
    collection is mainly autobiographical; we are led through the author's recounting of
    childhood, travels, motherhood, and finding love. There are also poems that explore the
    themes of aging and death"– Provided by publisher.
Identifiers: LCCN 2021000273 (print) | LCCN 2021000274 (ebook) | ISBN 9781944838898
    (paperback) | ISBN 9781944838904 (ebook)
Subjects: LCGFT: Poetry.
Classification: LCC PS3620.A23 A66 2021 (print) | LCC PS3620.A23 (ebook) |
    DDC 811/.6–dc23
LC record available at https://lccn.loc.gov/2021000273
LC ebook record available at https://lccn.loc.gov/2021000274

∞ This paper meets the requirements of ANSI/NISO Z39.48–1992 (Permanence of Paper).

Cover description: Background is a watercolor/ink graphic of birch trees turned on their
side. The space between the trees is varying shades of blue. On top right is the title:
Above the Birch Line. Center right is the subtitle: Poems. Lower right is the author name:
Pia Taavila-Borsheim. All text is set in a sans serif typeface.

Cover design by Latte Goldstein at River Design.

Praise for *Above the Birch Line*

"This book is a life long journey that begins, beautifully, with the request for a private existence ('Sometimes I want a life unseen, above the bookstore'); it asks for the life of attentiveness, a life of detail ('A small life, such as the one in which stew / bubbles on the stove and there is a wooden table / set with two bowls, two spoons, two mugs for milk / and thick napkins, white and folded. Bread bakes / while steam from the kettle clouds my glasses'). It is these details that give the poems their power, their imagistic depth and sweep. The poet does a beautiful job giving us the intimacy of perspective, the clarity of view, especially in the poems that look back, that deal with memory in poems that are narrative, but not prosy, lyrical but not needlessly inaccessible. There is a clear emotion running through these pages and the reader can relate to the voice of these poems.

There is also a beautiful economy of language in this book; for example:

Pale orchids bloom
    at the dappled windowsill.
Seven leaves watch me.

Much is said in just three lines in this poem. This is a nuanced, clear language, wherein imagery and emotion work hand in hand. Similar effect takes place in longer lyrics:

Presque Isle Landscape

A yellow bowl of blackberries,
a hydrangea blue plate,
white linen napkins.

A woman in a cotton dress
leans against a kitchen chair's
red oilcloth padding.

The wind off Lake Huron
skims her skin fine
as a cedar's barbed needles.

It really is this simple:
cool water to drink,
a screen in the window,

air enough to breathe.

The tension between what is said and unsaid is beautifully balanced
here. These are the strengths of this book."
—Ilya Kaminsky, author of *Deaf Republic*

"Pia Taavila-Borsheim's *Above the Birch Line* invokes a rich, resonant
past through the clear-eyed and compassionate lens of present wisdom.
From the silences of Deaf parents whose sign language speaks volumes,
to the tranquil summer days of Michigan rivers, outboard motors, and
hours lost to 'the lapping waves crowding one upon the other,' Taavila-
Borsheim writes with a sure touch and an inclusive vision. She is the
mother who bids a literal 'fare well' to the adult children who have left
home for the wider world, and she is the poet who wryly recalls former
loves while vividly chronicling travels to Colorado, Key West, Italy, and
Mangalore 'where, in moonlight, / musicians finger tablas, harmoniums,
/ singing and moaning to ancient ghazals.' *Above the Birch Line* offers
poems that are literal 'passages'—both journey and revelation—and those
who join this singular voyage will find themselves fortunate, indeed."
—Ned Balbo, author of *The Cylburn Touch-Me-Nots*

"The poems in *Above the Birch Line* are a harvest of arresting detail, entrancing musicality, and consistently evocative narrative. You'll find your eyes, ears, and heart revisiting (and marveling at) each line, image and stanza the way one pores over, say, a score by Claude Debussy. Pia Taavila-Borsheim's work honors her path, but she also takes us along on these vivid recollections. Lucky, lucky us."

—Reuben Jackson, author of *Scattered Clouds*

"Pia Taavila-Borsheim's *Above the Birch Line* is part poetic autobiography, part prayer book: a celebration of life in all its complicated beauty and a call for communion with the natural world. But it's also a guidebook—in sections moving from 'Notes from Childhood' to 'Notes Toward Death,' with important stops in between—to a lifelong journey of discovery. These poems offer us a careful contemplation of 'matters of heart and hand' from a sharp-eyed poet ready to capture each moment of wonder, fleeting as 'the flash of a cardinal's red wing / in a snowy forest.'"

—Matthew Thorburn, author of *The Grace of Distance*

"Haunting, aromatic, and atmospheric, Pia Taavila-Borsheim's poems reveal a coming to terms with the order and disorder of life and nature. At once panoramic and microscopic, they are moving and cinematic, shifting focus between details faraway and up close."

—Willy Conley, author of *Listening through the Bone*

"With imagistic precision and a rare generosity of spirit, *Above the Birch Line* confronts the sweep of a life—its joys and hungers and sorrows—while relishing the tiny details that somehow make all the difference: 'Pecans on waffles. / Purple lantana. Frothy ferns. / Dew . . . on coquina walls.' I was especially moved by this book's daring meditations on old age: the contradictory salve and stab of memory during 'this time of too much time' and yet the unexpected sweetness near the end."

—Anders Carlson-Wee, author of *The Low Passions*

"These poems are infected by—full of—water in all its guises. And this—the presence in nearly every poem of rain, snow, bays, creeks, clouds, huge lakes, rills on glass—is also *Above the Birch Line's* extraordinary strength. There is a clarity, a fluidity to these poems, a grace

vii

of registers from the very small to large, from childhood past old age, from early desire to late. And the poems hold within themselves a quiet urgency—to say a life, but a life in its various contexts and containers, a life deeply connected with the world. It is also a book of real, quiet, and, in its own way, ferocious maturity."

—Leslie Harrison, author of *The Book of Endings*

For David Borsheim, always and evermore my true north.

For my children and grandchildren: may you grow in strength and compassion, and may your lives be rich in love.

Contents

Above the Birch Line

Notes from Childhood

Norwegian Krone, 1891

My grandfather once gave me a silver coin
worth two *ore*. On one side, a rampant lion,
crowned, and on the back, the number two,
encircled by a wreath of linden leaves.

I carried this coin in my pocket every day,
going out and coming in, while playing,
reading in the town library,
waxing my skis, or meeting classmates to sing

every evening in the pine-ringed square.
I would slide my hand down to feel its rigid
edges, its markings raised in relief.
It smelled of his tobacco, his cologne.

It never slipped out, even as I hung, upside
down, in the tree I'd climbed, swaying
in the breeze off the fjord, nor when leaping
from rock to rock below the jagged cliffs.

The year stamped on its face was 1891,
the year of his birth. I give this coin now
to you, wrapped in purple tissue paper,
tied with an orange ribbon. As you move

about, as this coin jangles with its mates,
rubbing themselves smooth and shiny,
think of me. Touch its gleaming surface.
Finger its impressions. Keep it safe.

Down the Road

Here I am again, driving the long back roads,
my childhood in Michigan remembered anew.

First swim, first sail, first bluegill and bass,
first kiss, first heartache.

Yet the lakes, their deep blues, swing me full circle
now that the moons have pulled so many tides.

While I wade, minnows peck at my feet and ankles.
They dart like memories, dappled like Petoskey stones.

Tonight I will sleep on the ground beneath pine trees,
my tent pitched on yellow beach sand.

I will dream my Michigan dream: that I am flying,
my legs long stilts stretched to the ground below,

where my mother waters her geraniums and my father
guns the Evinrude, a beer in his bearlike paw. He opens

the throttle's throat as he takes off, out into the inlet,
his red cap fading from view. My siblings play in the next

lot, tossing the ball back and forth. They're dead now,
but in my dream they are tow-headed and kind,

tossing bobbers into my bicycle basket, rolling
cheese and bread balls, handing me hooks to bait.

They let me watch as they gut the catch, wiggling
the entrails to frighten me. When I wake, I swear,

there is no blood on my hands. Only the moon stares
down, the lapping waves crowding one upon the other.

November, 1963

The first time I saw my mother
cry, her tears fell into a blue bowl,
splayed and pooled on cookie dough,
the dark chips jagged and shiny.

No salt needed now, she signed,
her gaze fixed on the flickering screen,
the TV perched on a shelf near the sink.
In the kitchen that morning, silence

cooled linoleum floors, my bare feet
pricked with goose bumps, achy.
Mother sagged on the chrome stool,
arms crossed above her belly.

Later I watched as his wife turned to climb
the back seat, a purse on her arm,
her perfect pillbox hat, to gather his head
to her cheek, to reach for something

already gone, her eyes frantic, her eyes
already bright with grief. My mother's eyes,
too, gone from me, our shopping, our baking
set aside for the day, the blue bowl

beading up when the fire went out.

Ortiz' Dry Cleaners

An open, stonework terrarium clings
to the entryway wall. Salamanders
skitter along the piped-in streams,
the pebbles green with algae.

Pops Ortiz, a lizard on one shoulder,
leans across the counter to take my ticket.
He presses a button. Garments swirl,
then climb a track line to the rafters.

I wait for my father's shirts.
Pops points to a photo of his son hanging on the wall,
cock-eyed, near the penny candy machine.
Handsome boy, no? You will marry him, no?

Pops sizes me up, his eyes fixed on
the parts that count. Clacking rollers
grind to a halt. Pops sets the hangers
on the pickup rack, palms my cash,

offers the receipt. When I try to reach
for it, he grabs my wrist, hissing through
mossy teeth, "Don't be so choosy, chica."
I turn to run without dad's shirts,

squash a newt too close to the door,
and bolt four blocks home before breathing.
My father, startled from his evening newspaper,
looks at me with eyebrows raised.

On the Au Sable River

In my boat: a rod and reel, some bobbers and hooks,
a stringer and sunscreen, my floppy hat.

A cool mist rose and shrouded the shoreline.
The oarlocks creaked, turning in the gunwales.

I rowed downstream to the mouth of the river
as if I thought it had something to tell me.

With worms and minnows, I lured
the smallmouth bass to strike. Again

and again, the bobber pulled under.
The reel clicked as it slowly spun.

A half-hour later, I'd caught my legal limit;
their upper scales shimmered at dawn.

Then, the concrete slab, the sharpened knife,
the spray-nozzled hose hanging nearby.

How smooth to cut along their white bellies,
their deadened eyes still staring, accusing.

The fish yielded to the crimson slits. Their guts
spooled out, their notched tails stilled, I sliced

filets and washed away debris. I wished for
so clean a death, so fast and efficient.

I wrapped the cutlets in wax paper, layered
them in ice, and drove home as the sun ascended.

Dipped in egg, then dredged in bread crumbs,
their battered flesh sizzled in the pan.

Flag Pole

Today I touched my father's gravestone
with the flat of my hand, as if he were merely
feverish and not dead, not underground
here in the Sequatchie River Valley.

I picture him back home at the kitchen table,
trying to hear a Benny Goodman record
through thick headphones, leaning forward,
nursing a Stroh's and a travel magazine,

or standing at the stove, stirring a saucepan,
heating up new maple butter to pour out
on the snow in pretzel-shaped candy,
a Lucky Strike dangling from his lips.

I picture him stumbling down the stairs
drunk, cursing in sign language, mean,
smashing things at the workbench,
breaking windows with his hammer.

I see him throwing his keys at my mother's apron,
firing off a rifle, pocking the fridge. I see
his head in the back of a disappearing squad car
as my mother clings to the doorframe.

For years there was small news of him:
the clocks he fixed, a new wife, an address
somewhere in California. Then the checks arrived,
federal, the death benefit received.

Now I am sixty-five. Odd, how blood is thicker
than memory. After months of searching, I find him.
I come to this field to see the summer scrum
of a mower in the distance, to brush the cuttings away.

Notes for My Former Loves

Two Birds

Across our northern skies, two birds
charge and wheel, the smaller sleek
in hot pursuit. Perhaps the larger

skulked to raid the newborn nest.
Perhaps a tuft of food its beaked
desire lured. Whatever the cause

of this flight's rage, they grapple, peck,
fall, and swoop. The chaser nips
the other's tail, ignores the odds,

defying physics, brave in sheer
revenge, aloft. I watch them wing
throughout the morn, then turn to walk

long-rutted fields. Briars, hawthorn
rise to snag. Their gnarled beauty
holds a single feather, black.

Climbing the Bluff

All day long I hiked through the woods
on snowshoes made of leather and lath, climbed
a ravine whose snowy banks and drifting peaks
lay steep against the trunks of pines.

Black-eyed cardinals watched from branches,
tucked their heads when the wind kicked up
crystals of icy flakes that lashed their beaks.
The birds followed me, red daubs on the trail.

I walked on to inhabit stillness, silence,
to calm love's disappointment. When I reached
the cliff top's knob, I turned and gazed across
the frost-tipped valley. I studied the blue bay:

its curving shoreline frozen, its chop white-capped
and rough. I stood there for hours, till the lines
of drizzling sweat dried, till the sun fell from its
fading sky and the villagers' lights began to gleam.

Throughout the dark descent, gray wolves
called in yips and wails, great rolling howls.
The torsos of trees, still stark against the white,
made clear the path below. I cried out, too.

Wake

What do you fear, wayward wanderer?
Is it the loss of your sweetheart's gaze?
Or that you will go mad by morning?
Is it the grave with its lovelorn vault?

Shelter in sorrow's rock-mouth cave
behind a scrim of fog, barely visible—
Look out over these vales of woe
and tell me true—what makes you tremble?

Can you defy the raindrop's erosion?
Or daylight's departure, fleet-footed
and cruel? How will the night's
long loon cry hollow your core?

Ponder the sky's vast illusion,
the length of your own shadow.
Then, teach me not to weep.

Sherry Glasses

In a china shop window, two
petite crystal goblets shimmer,
refracting late-day sun. Even now
I know. Even as they turn, prismatic
in our hands, even as we admire

their wreaths of finely etched leaves,
their slender ankles, the discs of their feet,
I know I will break one, only one,
and ruin this pair, end this coupledom.

It will happen when I wash them.
After sponging warm suds and a hot
water rinse, I will set each one to dry,
upturned on its head in a wire basket
on the sink's rippled drain board.

Sure enough, one will slide into the other
just so—just a tap, really, and shatter its stem.
The break-point shard will gleam in its cruelty.
I will know then as I know now no glue can mend
this fragile piece, this ragged edge.

There will come no moment of lifting
to our lips even one bright, shared,
bittersweet drop. I will gather the remains.
With care, I will toss them in the trash.

Marriage

A floorboard creaks, cries,
     despite our best intentions
to avoid that plank.

After He Leaves

Right about now, eight months later,
I imagine my ex- at his kitchen table,
listening to the radio in his underwear and socks.

A song comes on and he'd like to dance,
to take a turn across the living room, down the hall,
only there's no one to put his arms around,

no true love with whom he might lift a glass
or digest the news. No one who could cause
his heart to quicken in that massive chest.

Right about now, I imagine him doodling
or filling in the spaces of a crossword puzzle,
filling in the gaps with a woman here and there

who will delight him for about as long as it takes
to change the sheets, which he will launder
and hang to dry, flapping from a stretched line.

Here at home I roll out the dough for lemon tarts,
season roasted potatoes and rosemary chicken,
grind coffee from Arabica beans in the Cuisinart

he bought last November. The gears and blades
growl in sharp precision, the grind spilling
into a plastic cup I wash while listening

to the radio without static, a clear signal
to dance to on a starlit night, and I will
nestle in fresh sheets, mid-bed, alone.

The Internet Dating Game

Bachelor No. 1:
I own a pistol, two rifles, voted for Nixon, and breed Great Danes.

Bachelor No. 2:
I see my psychotherapist four times a week.
We talk about my mother. And my sister.

Bachelor No. 3:
Have you heard the one about the rabbi and the priest?
You have? Four times already? From me?

Bachelors Nos. 4, 5, and 6:
My favorite film is *Smokey and the Bandit.*

Bachelor No. 7:
I was unlucky in love. I finally divorced that damn bitch in Louisville.

Bachelor No. 8:
Baby, what's your bra size?

Bachelor No. 9:
Ooooh, you sound nice.
I'm an Adolf type in search of Mata Hari.
Chains are involved.
Call me.

Frame

Pale orchids bloom
      at the dappled windowsill.
Seven leaves watch me.

Notes from My Travels

Longitude

Once, along the earth's wide curve, I set
my trajectory and wandered, parallel
to its axial spine, molten as its core.

Now, a globe in my study spins.
Pastel nations blur to a single continent,
mottled by seas whose brine tastes of tears.

I brush my palms against the world
and hope its lines of latitude, magnetic north,
will show me next the way to you.

I pinpoint your bed, six time zones hence,
with a plotter's precision. You rise from sleep
to take my call. *Hello*, I say. *Who's this?* you ask.

Lost

Out on Lake Huron, I raise the keel,
tie down jibs, lash the spar and rudder.
The anchor reels out, heavy on its chain.
My radio rasps as a gull climbs overhead,
immune to matters of heart and hand.

Board games and jigsaw puzzles,
their pieces gone missing, line the shelves.
The galley's loaded with provisions,
but no beneficence lies on board,
the first mate's absence obvious.

I look at weather maps, arrowed charts,
the sky, and try to set a forward destination.
There's nowhere to go, no fish to lure
as the sun slowly slides beneath
the waterline: shores of vapor, haze.

At the Ferry

Near Ludington, I stop for purple lilacs, for three young plants
in black plastic pails, wrapped in trash bags, gently placed
and buckled in on my car's back seat. I crack the windows
and drive into town on the side streets, past prim Victorians,
the elementary, the downtown shops, already busy with tourists.

Lines of school children stand outside the firehouse door,
clutching tickets for Sno-Cones, angling for a chance to heft the hose,
to wear the lightweight headgear, emblazoned, red, to slide swiftly
down the gleaming pole. I see them bicker and jostle to be first.

I park in the waterfront lot and linger dockside, feeding the gulls.
A group of bicyclists gathers at the gate. Its leader consults his GPS,
his watch. They open sandwiches wrapped in foil. One of them squats
on his haunches and hunkers down to wait. The hours pass.

The launch finally comes into view and moors. With everyone on board,
the boatman hauls in his ramp and heaves away to guide his group
across the blue expanse, to pull the whistle, to set his sights beyond.
I wave goodbye and hope to see him late next spring when lilacs bloom.

The back-seat plants track the sun as day wears on. I think of where
I'll plant them, how the summer's rain will soon sustain them
once I am home. As night falls, I give them a drink from my travel cup,
then enter the roadway, my headlights steady on the lane.

Colorado Farewell

Pale aspen leaves, lined,
      lying in my open hand,
fly off in the breeze.

Thirst

At the southern tip of Key West, beachside,
a café opens its groaning shutters to palm trees.
Pigeons rise and flutter toward the sand
where land and ocean meet, of one mind.

Tourists stroll the long blocks as a man
in gold lamé bicycles down the lane,
a blue parrot squatting on his shoulder.
Rheumy-eyed shrimpers congregate in parks.
Jamaican nannies rouse to their charges.

At the other end of Duval Street, a bakery's
blue awnings overlook the Gulf. A lizard
climbs the door jamb. Pecans on waffles.
Purple lantana. Frothy ferns.
Dew glistens on coquina walls.

All this tropical blooming. All this moisture.
Not one single drop of you.

Massage Therapy

Votives flicker. Buddha watches,
golden voyeur, from his wicker stand.
The sheet luffs across my back,

light as the master's breath.
I close my eyes, my mind adrift.
His hands will have to do for now.

As he rubs out kink and knot,
drums away at ridge and marl,
my muscles yield to knead and touch

to hum in softened symmetry.
Passageways, furrows, nerve endings,
grief, all lean into his fingers, elbows, palms.

Silkened in oils—of lemon balm and sage—
my thirsty dermas blush. When he lifts
the sheet for me to flip, I turn, graceful

as a seal who spins through piano
music sea. He strokes and skims my hips,
lines the length of my limbs, asks,

*Are you too tender? Is this too much, too hard,
too deep?* He purls my chakras and toes,
circles my ankles, moves back and forth

then holds my feet, silent and still.
The room is filled with all that's between us,
and all that is not. Then, the doorknob clicks.

Piazza

Moonlight creeps through linden leaves,
casts long shadows on sidewalk slab.

The last train's passengers hurry by
(newspapers tucked under their arms),

chatting of wine and weekend plans.
Once their goodbyes dissipate,

a silence settles in, sweet and lonely.
Under a café table, a cat cleans herself,

stretching and licking, certain in the dark,
in its intimate protections.

I sit on a wrought iron bench to mull over
the day's events, nursing a drink

and the closed buds of tulips,
the bits of paper littering the grass.

Soon enough I'll climb the steps
to my rented room, turn the iron key

in the great brass lock. For now, I coax
a pigeon to cluck, to sing to me tonight.

Mangalore

Suppose the banyan tree did not twist upon itself
and that its roots did not gnarl across the pathway
or that monkeys no longer stole the fruit off my plate,
mating without regard to partner, place, or time.

Temples of the gods reveal their carnal pleasures
carved in grotesque relief, the lovers entwined
in panel after panel. As I climb seven hundred steps
to see the Jain statue in all its male glory, I am

reminded of all that I lack. Even the air sighs
with steam and thick heavings; even coconut
milk from its hairy shell sticks to the tongue,
nearly bitter to swallow, not enough to quench.

I lift a bottle of Limca from its ice-cubed tub
only to watch it burst in my hand in the too-hot
day. My host runs for a towel and dabs at me,
trying to avoid what he calls those "sacred spaces."

Frangipani blossoms haunt the village square,
lift to the roof tops where, in moonlight,
musicians finger tablas, harmoniums,
singing and moaning to ancient ghazals.

I climb down to the livestock pens, lean against
tough, warm hides. The breathing of cows shivers
up my arms. I'm drawn to the smell of hay
and manure; a pail of cream cools in the corner.

I See Horses

In evening air, the musk of dampening flanks
lifts from the brood to nostrils that flare.
The young ones practice their approach,

hooves slipping off as she moves away to tear
grass from sloping lawns. She urinates.
Drawn to her crouching, the yearlings try again,

but the mare turns tail, bares teeth, nips.
At the lower gate, a farmhand off-loads the service
stud, a roan stallion, kicking in the rig.

A ramp is reeled out and sandbagged. Blindfolded,
he's backed down the chute, led to her pen,
unmasked, turned loose. He crisscrosses

the paddock, traversing fence lines in fleet
navigation. At the window, I lean out over
the sill transfixed, watching, waiting.

Underground

Let me wait as the crocus waits,
folded, petal upon petal,
the wrapped core still alive,
still pulsing, yet content to count,
the snow's mantle oddly soothing
above the bulb's curled destiny.

Then, when the sun trains its gaze
upon the earth's horizon,
when nestlings rustle,
I will send up a shoot,
a spire of fiery purple
to glisten in spring rain.

Notes from Motherhood

A Mother's Lament

The children launched from my womb
no longer chart the amniotic shore

nor does the milk-smell pull them
toward the heart whose blood

once thrust in their veins. Gone
are the uplifted hands. Light

is the weight in my arms, mere air
as I paw and grasp to hold them near.

Now, they walk this earth tall and sure
of their straying destinations. Now

I am no more to them than a recipe
on the phone. They were only loaned

to me for a season, and I have sent them
on their way. They don't look back.

They're gone, the chores completed,
the groceries bought and paid for,

bagged up, brought home to sit
on the shelf, to cool in the fridge.

O self-pity, you are a cruel demon
who rises in this time of too much time.

Root

My children, I stand here before you,
my skin no more than leaves shirred off

in wind or dangling in long shreds
like seed pods from catalpa trees.

Strip the bark. Under its decaying crust
you will find striations, the stippling

of woodpeckers drilling for bugs.
At its core, the trunk may be rotten.

Still, some sap may come,
some sweetness yet to rise,

to surge into veined capillaries:
a blossom here or there.

Soldier Son

When my son entered the war,
all he wanted was to clean his rifle
at the kitchen table, showing me
the moving parts, their deadly functions.

He was in love with tanks
and helicopters, weaponry
of any kind. Brutal, he became
brutal and distanced himself

from me without care, without
looking back. Such a far cry
from the universe our eyes
held when I nursed him,

such a long way to run from
the arms that once cradled him.
What can a mother do?
I see him now, a man who drinks,

who bickers with his wife,
who maintains that wall,
that silence, that sheer
immutability. Mute.

Hovering

Son with the acid-laced pupils,
what hollow thing eats at you?

Is your mind/body meandering
nothing more than youthful gaming?

Or does death knock at your ribcage,
its filthy fingers picking at your mortar?

Stand down from this ledge
before the quicksand covers you

and I can no longer cup your fleeting pulse.

Fare Well to Six Children

Live on and be grateful.
   Sing, for day breaks anew,
even as sorrow slings
   its shadows on the lawn.

Release all prisoners,
   that storehouse of regret.
Say *No* to your captors
   when asked to weep again.

Heed the new life calling
   like the lone hawk that soars.
When suns ascend the skies,
   think of me, elated.

Break into flame-red blooms,
   your petals thrust outward,
your yellow filaments
   waving bravely in wind.

Then shall I rest, my bones
   blanching along some shore,
pulled out to sea in bits
   of lace-like foam, so light.

Notes to David

Thunder Bay

On the beach, a man is sleeping. All morning long
he fished from shore, casting his line again and again
out into Lake Huron, the hook floating back, empty.

Behind him, the yellow land stretches into a stand
of birch trees and ferns, their undersides dotted
with black-beaded spores. I've watched him take

his daily nap for months now, from a splintered
plank on a picnic table near a campfire ring.
His chest rises and falls as he sleeps. When he shifts,

a sheath of sand rasps up his thighs and spine,
the mica glinting in his hair. I wonder what his name is,
why he's alone. My gaze follows from afar,

tracks his every move as the sun splays across
the jetty and marina. On the day he sees me,
he'll prop up on one elbow, his head cocked

at some oblique angle, as a frond turns toward the sky.
He'll raise an eyebrow, a question mark's curl
like a fiddlehead fern. I gather twigs and shells.

Chance

I wish I could write you
a love song on parchment paper,
blue ink applied with a quill.
I'd fold it in fourths,
leave it under your cup.
You'd find it hours later,
search for its author.

I'd fill your sky with little birds.
One would land on your shoulder
and sing to you all day.

I'd hold your toes like cotton socks
soft and heathery, the ones you pull on
before those wrinkled leather shoes.
As you walk here and there,
you'd feel me with you.

I wish to drop gold coins on you,
shimmering in mid-air,
turning in the sun like maple leaves.

I wish you had a need for me like air.
Essential, thoughtless, easy.
I wish I had the nerve to say,
Here I am.

Instead, I hide behind shy thoughts,
this feckless page.
Imaginary lover,
find me.

Wisp

Come to me like a bell on a breeze,
quietly. In an unexpected moment,

like the flash of a cardinal's red wing
in a snowy forest.

Or like a memory, unbidden,
private, yet to which you are wholly present.

Come to me as you will
in the middle of the night,

creeping along the floorboards
and walls, silent and stealthy.

Like lilacs in full bloom,
resplendent with each bud

opening to the air,
infuse the shorelines of longing.

There's nothing to discuss,
endlessly expectant.

That calm, that easy,
without preconception.

Come to me as you will,
your cap in your hand,

your bike against my cabin,
your breath in my ear.

Shopping

In the international market, a woman is asking
for cardamom pods, chilies, those lovely yellow
mustard seeds. In her buggy are chicken thighs,
chard, lemons the size of my fist. Her toddler's

legs dangle and kick as he eyes slices of pineapple
and mango, clutching a stuffed lion and a pear.
He looks at me, shyly smiling, so I offer my hand.
His dimpled fingers, their pale white nails,

rest in my palm, sticky and sweet. While I swoon
and praise him, his eyelashes, thick and black,
sweep and close. His mother laughs. She tells me
he is a charmer to whom all the ladies are drawn.

In that moment, I think of another market,
a bookstore, where I saw you at the podium.
After your reading, a clutch of women asked
for your autograph, pressed against you as if

so doing staked a claim. I sat still in the back row,
took in your words of seduction, your poems
full of invitation, your voice a mahogany saxophone.
I was swept away, yearning for you in my woolen wrap,

my bag of fruit slumped on the chair beside me.
Above the many heads vying, you looked across the rows
to find me waiting. Your gaze was lovely, grey with
dark blue flecks, questioning. *Yes*, I nodded. *Yes*.

Proposal

If we should touch beneath the table,
flushing up surprised, rare birds
lifting, stealthy, under skin,
in what barbed moment might we meet?

If I should take your offered hand,
lined and brown, slow to touch,
to thresh and hone my cheek's parched heat,
what chance might soar in these bright days?

If you should leave before the birds
have plundered all from craggy banks,
before the rushing creeks recede,
what dark, soft rain could wash me clean?

Roofline

A woodpecker drills the gutter, relentless.
Her red head blurs as her beak, thin
jackhammer, bores the hole more hollow.

She's on a mission, urgent, efficient.
I would love you like that,
single-minded, sure-footed.

Her flecked feathers knit and fray
in winter's ice-laced wind. I hear her.
Obedient to nature's dictate, tireless,

she knocks.

Psalm

When he sings to me in Hebrew,
the love songs and the prayers,
refrains of working in the fields,
I need the fullness of his voice,
its tenor deep, resounding.

His measure fills the living room.
Ferns and curtains sway
to each sweet note. Lyrics lift
as he takes another breath,
tilts back his head, closes his eyes.
His singing warms like embers
flaring in the fireplace.

Desire

From knotted rhizomes,
from the soil and loam,
purple iris plants branched
in my garden last spring.

I cut some with my knife,
the gash at each bulb's rising
pulp-like and white.
I brought an armful of stalks

into the house, filled a glass vase
nearly full, and set them on my desk.
Backlit by an office lamp,
their veins pulsed in the just-

opened blooms, in the stamens
and pistils. I thought I could see
their vascular structure, how water
transpired via xylem and leaf.

When I ran my hand along
one stem, it seemed to vibrate,
to welcome touch, sensation.
Its cells seemed to blush, as I do

when my lover brushes my skin:
a slight shiver, an inhalation,
then the full-on rush, from core to brain,
of common conflagration.

Marriage to a Widower

This morning, at breakfast, my husband regales me
with stories and poems, bits and pieces of yesterday's
news, so many memories crowding his mind.

Yes, it's sweet, but throughout his long litany,
the word *we* rears its hissing head, and I am left
to wonder: to what degree are the dead really dead,

how much more than an urn of ashes under
the snow, under the marble bench engraved
with both their names? I've pulled out my best

recipes, my checkbook, my most alluring gowns.
I've lotioned my limbs, made warm the marital bed,
but who can compete with this ghost from the grave?

I find her in the hallway, her ear pressed to the wall.
She creeps into the bedroom. Above our lovemaking
she whispers, staring down at me from the airy ceiling.

Wednesday Mornings

He bends to the task, clipping
his father's toe nails, the old
man prone on his recliner,
a quilt tucked to his chin.

I watch, from across the room,
the slow, steady working, shards
of yellowed nails jetting
through the heated air.

Then, the cleaning of his hearing
aids, the tiny brush employed,
rinsed: the minute seashell,
electronic wizardry, restored.

When all is done, my sweetheart
stands to take the offered hand,
lined and cracking, to pat the quilt,
to kiss his father's shining head.

For David

Off the street, past the corner guitar man, we turn left into the long arcade.
Its glass-topped ceiling dribbles the last rain as evening slows the clouds.

Shops line the walkway, small flags draped at each bell-clapped door.
Here we find perfumes, stationery, that silk tie you've wanted,

or cinnamon rolls at the baker's, steaming up the window.
A constable sits his horse, clopping down the cobbled lane.

A child flits past, a clump of ribbons streaming from her hand
while a gaggle of teens, furtive, smirks at us, at our arm-in-arm gait,

our middling paunches. No matter. We amble on.
A wisp of curry scents the damp air as you reach for me, your hands

in my hair, your lips on my cheek. In the near-dark, we sixty-somethings
still grow breathless, laugh out loud, our voices startling the birds, who rise.

Delayed Gratification

Late-life husband, practice kindness
for I've arrived ill-used, I'm afraid.
When I cock my head in disbelief
of your loving, lusty proclamations,

exercise patience, leniency, for the trip
to you has been tangled and sad. Fear not
my tentative responses. Keep looking for me,
holed up in one cove or another, curled.

I will soon shed this second skin, will send my shield
spinning on its backside. Until then, continue to caress,
your bemused and happy gaze lingering upon me.
Soon shall I wake as one long lost: hungry, thirsty, glad.

Solstice: Still Life with Husband

The sky is now a watercolor mist
swept with gray pastels, clouds.

On the branches of a black cherry,
liquid lines of bronzing sunset
slip, as though a painter's fox-tail brush
were tipped with gold mercury, filigree.

Small rivulets of rays seem to ooze
along the arching limbs to drizzle
and gild the tree's barren crown.

On a park bench above the pond,
we've set down our books to view
this sight, its shining mystery.

Notes Toward Aging

While Weeding

A dandelion's fluff scatters, its seed bolls lifted in wind,
their destinations unknown and rocky, most like.

My neighbor calls again, her words repetitive, aimless
sleepwalker talk, heedless of its rambling ways.

Shall I call a doctor or her son? Who knows which way
our failing bodies will plunge: the long trajectory

or an imminent demise? I wonder how my frame will
fare, what meanderings my mind will undergo.

Will I linger, or will I derail at a sudden stop,
a stalk of grass beneath the mower's blade?

I watch one puff pod float along, its cloud aloft,
its last ascent, drifting before the fall, its pointed

aril poised to rake the soil. I wish it safe landing,
that its roots grow deep, its jagged leaves tenacious.

From Car to Schwinn and Back Again

In that moment, you say *yes*, you will drive down
that unknown road, a back road, even though
you don't know where it goes and time is short.

You are not instantly rewarded, as the strip
malls and parking lots are slow to give way,
slow to end their hold on consciousness.

Soon, the pine groves thicken, the hills roll.
The two-lane curves beneath an old-growth
canopy, and you think yourself a child again,

bicycling home from the lake, or a ball game,
the sun slanting through to the forest floor ferns.
You keep pedaling, sure that you're alone, sure

that this world exists for only you, each furled frond
lifting its head, its black dots of spore for you alone,
there in your t-shirt and shorts and barefoot, yes, barefoot,

your tanned legs lean and muscular, the rubber lever
ready to ring its bell on the handlebars as your spokes,
shimmering, spin and spin, the red reflector

bringing up the rear. Before suburbia interjects,
you stand and balance, let go the frame, tilt
your head so your hair streams like a flag.

But it is only a car, after all, and you have a husband
and bills to pay, a dog to walk, and lines to stay
within, yellow lines, solid in your lane.

Main Street

Sometimes I want a life unseen, above the bookstore,
a small life, lined with shelves of novels and poems,
a life of sinking my hands into soft, grey wool,
a knitting project, the needles clacking.

At the window, snow pelts, in falling light,
the blackbirds that arrow eastward, across
the bay where the lighthouse flares its fan.
A small life, such as the one in which stew

bubbles on the stove and there is a wooden table
set with two bowls, two spoons, two mugs for milk,
and thick napkins, white and folded. Bread bakes
while steam from the kettle clouds my glasses.

You know this life, the one I want. It is devoid
of clatter, of clamor's insistence. Instead, it is
a life of red rain boots poised at the doorstep,
of a handful of friends and good lines in the writing,

a life in which the postman, huffing up the stairs,
hands me a packet of letters bound in cotton cording,
their messages tender, of good hope and cheer. A life
worth its silence, its simple, sacred yearnings.

Diskobolos

My students now study the sculptor and statue
marking externals, proportion and scale.
We talk of the casting, of bronze, wax, or stone,
of chisel and bit, of angle and stance,
the trick of believing it moved or it spoke.
We ponder intention, the artist's technique,
all the while confronting the shock of our
selves looking in mirrors, the false masks, the pose.

Oh, to be naked, truly stripped down, exposed,
where one's inner essence resides on the skin
in veins of fine marble, in muscle and pore.
I step off the platform, regard my life's work,
and take up the hammer to smash things
to bits, brutal and glad. The students gasp.

First Drafts

"... in the scribbled first drafts of my life ..."

David Mura, *Grandfather-in-Law*

Hasty, scribbled, fly-legged marks,
nearly illegible now, lie those earlier
versions of the self I've become.

Like scrabbled tiles falsely aligned,
jumbled along the player's side
of life's board, its numbered squares ...

One word can turn all scoreboards,
and there can be winners, in the end,
despite shifts, jumping ships, cut adrift

or leaping into air à la Matisse.
A woman's heart, pliable, red,
is likely as not to strike gold.

We love hit or miss until, at last,
a multitude of revisions leads
to pay dirt. Listen to me.

I've known the ill-met fit,
the discomfiture of passion's cell,
and I can say with full voice

that now the angst was worth
every penny, every sleepless night,
every agony and brokenness.

Now I find solace in the honey bee
and bird, in the spring-fed lake,
in your steady gaze, your shoes by the door.

For Aging Couples

As I lie here in your arms, eyes closed, the ruined world pulls away.
Lips, skin, touch, and breath become the one true realm, pricked
by pinpoints of light in black space, the rays of desire expanding.

A shaft of moonlight hits your jawline, silvers your chest hair.
Your gaze meets mine as our limbs entangle. The pulsing vortex
draws us in, hastens our need. We turn and spin, spooling in wave

after wave of vast implosion. Once our heartbeats slow and soften,
I tuck my head beneath your chin. You raise your hands to stroke
my head and start to sing: a paean, a lullaby, a dirge.

March Morning

It seems I've been granted another day to live,
as has the goldfinch in his brightening robe.
He pecks at the feeder for black sunflower seeds.
I watch from the porch, my coffee cup in hand.

The essence of things is what interests me now.
What can be felt, seen, or known? What of salt,
so sharp on the tongue? What of those quests for
which we thirst along wide lanes, or bays, or hills?

I seek the day's design, its import or beneficence,
much as the sun scans the corners of this room.
I seek the raw, revealing message, the compass points
whose needles shiver toward the North's sure pull.

While my love still lies asleep, I plan our menus,
the savory and sweet, the succulent and plain.
We'll run errands in town, our packages wrapped
in white paper and twine, the butcher's fat cat

stretched out in the window. Sated with all our
provision, rich and small, we'll talk at the table,
draw out each thought, each lasting look and touch,
then settle in to bed as birds nest, the moon ascendant.

Presque Isle Landscape

A yellow bowl of blackberries,
a hydrangea-blue plate,
white linen napkins.

A woman in a cotton dress
leans against a kitchen chair's
red oilcloth padding.

The wind off Lake Huron
skims her skin fine
as a cedar's barbed needles.

It really is this simple:
cool water to drink,
a screen in the window,

air enough to breathe.

Notes Toward Death

We Birds in Love

The trilling call and hoot, the loon's cry:
      a warble, chatter, taunt,

or a warning sputtered branch to branch.
      Why do we ever trumpet and shout?

Is it joy of a morning? The "I am"
      proclamation?

Do simple shifts in tail or wind
      make us caw,

or will death's shrill hand tune
      our chords to thrumming?

O, choking hack in the throat's long hollow,
      which summons shall we gladly seize?

Sail

Before first light I slip the sailboat's prow
into the river's languid inlet.
Clear water runnels flow along the bow,
the air so still no feather ruffs.

I push off with one small kick, grasp
the gunnels, find my seat above
the hull's sure planking. The rasp
of turnbuckle, of masthead sheeting

sound across the pleating wake. I row
three strokes, then slide the keel into its well,
tie down the tiller, check all fallow
landmarks. Paddling out into the bay,

I feel a brisk wind billow. Cleat routes
loosed, the rigging falls, the sail
unfurls. I free the tiller, come about,
and head to where the sun awaits.

My lantern bobs atop the spar.
Harbor buoys, geese, and ducks trail
behind. Turtles nest on sandy bars
while soft waves lap and curl, lap and curl.

Content to hold the ropes this lightly,
now I seek the mid-stream depths.
A heron lifts in morning flight:
my luffing sail, her plumage blue.

To My Biographer

When I am an old woman, bent and gaunt,
I'll wear my hair piled high on my head,
a bun held in place with long, grey pins.
You'll think you know about me. Come.

Each week I pull the coupled chains,
set slim weights to rise and fall to start
this grandfather clock, the pendulum's arc,
until one day when the works will freeze up.

You'll open the etched glass door, slide
out a walnut panel, poke among the gears
and chimes, the clinging spider webs.
The machinery will hang up, halt

on the bulk of an envelope, its corner
stuck where the frame meets the base.
You'll tug at it, but it will not budge. You'll twist
to read the handwriting, the address

scrawled in cursive, in black, spindly lines.
You'll search the case for a lock whose
key, as you turn it in the tumbler, will
click in its chamber. There, below

brass fittings and filigreed cogs,
you'll find lost letters, hundreds of them,
neatly stacked, creased vellum,
dated across eighty-odd years,

all of them with foreign postage.
Some bear the detritus of silverfish;
some are illegible. Those you can
read will make you weep.

Toward Death

Soon my breath will blanch;
      my bones shall fly as ash-filled
motes of dust in air.

Passage

Bury me above the birch line,
where the pale bark curls
and the round leaves curve to serrated points.

Bury me below the towering pines
where the ragged cones fall
and icy needles hang heavy on the branch.

Or let my bones blanch in August sun,
pulled out from shore by starving birds
who wing away on high. Only then

shall I be at peace, this longing
brought to bank, lying still at last
under drifting snow, the lakeward winds.

Haiku Sequence: Night Watch

Meant for the gnawing,
       the meat and the marrow bone.
Live for the feasting.

     ~

Little frog, singing
       in the rain, joy attends you
under the stone step.

     ~

Elgar's *Nimrod* soars.
       I'm a clarinetist, twelve,
first chair, lone weeper.

     ~

Sprinkler heads skitter
       above the newly laid sod.
We watch from windows.

     ~

Empty milk bottles
       line the hallway shelf, the glass
gently green, clinking.

     ~

Tiny, pink, threaded
       cap, heart-shaped perfume bottle—
slight squeak, twisting off.

     ~

Creeping past my door,
       a young cat yowls at the moon.
Neighbors' lights come on.

     ~

A garret, pine trees—
       slant light through dormer windows—
a pine bed, plain desk.

I bend to the task,
       listen for the heart's desire,
type night-long lyrics.

The birds of morning call.
        Crumpled sheets fill the basket—
nine lines remain.

                    ~

A driver slices the air.
        The golf ball's *thwock*:
its rattle in the cup.

                    ~

Cars, in streetlight, nudge
        dark curbs: wet asphalt, strewn leaves.
Couples hurry by.

Lamps in high windows
        cast shadows through mottled trees.
I walk the dark stretch

of arching branches,
        alone in my need to name
the night air, alone.

                    ~

A baby cries in
        someone's neighboring house.
We sleepy mothers wake.

                    ~

In the door, his keys
        clank and jangle. The morning
tryst trails from his shirt.

                    ~

In my lover's eyes,
        the world's barbarism lurks:
slits for irises.

                    ~

Time to make a move.
        This snake slithers in tall grass,
shedding skin, revealed.

                    ~

Beaks fly out my mouth.
       Turquoise and teal, the feathers
furl. In flight, they caw.

~

He stood before me,
       humbled, penitent. I raised
his chin to kiss him.

~

Like a girl who lifts
       her skirts and crosses the creek,
we try again, love.

~

His words hung like fruit
       dangling from persimmon trees,
bruised and out of reach.

~

The heart knocks about
       in its empty casing, wants
only to beat on.

~

O, full moon, I stare
       into your pale sphere: haunting,
luminous, distant.

Winter Night

A sliver of moon,
        transparent as a widow's
fingernail, hanging—

Acknowledgments

I am grateful to the editors of the following magazines, journals, anthologies, and presses for publishing the following poems:

32 Poems   Lost

The Adirondack Review   Piazza
                                        Longitude

Alliterati Magazine   Proposal

Apricity Magazine   Norwegian Krone, 1891

Backbone Mountain Review   After He Leaves
                                        Massage Therapy

Bear River Review   At the Ferry
                                        Fare Well to Six Children
                                        On the Au Sable River

Birmingham Poetry Review   Mangalore

Blue Lyra Review   Chance
                                        March Morning

Conflictus Review   Hovering

Cumberland River Review	While Weeding
Duende	From Car to Schwinn
Fredericksburg Literary Review	Marriage to a Widower
Gargoyle	Toward Death
The Journal of Kentucky Studies	Sail
Linden Avenue Literary Journal	Root
Love Poems	Psalm
Measure: A Review of Formal Poetry	Marriage
Michigan Quarterly Review	Down the Road
Mojave River Review	Wisp
Moon on the Meadow: Collected Poems	November, 1963 The Internet Dating Game
Mother Mail	A Mother's Lament
Northern Virginia Review	Wednesday Mornings
Pennsylvania Literary Review	I See Horses Ortiz' Dry Cleaners Sherry Glasses To My Biographer
Poetry Repairs	Thirst
The Poetry Storehouse	Climbing the Bluff We Birds in Love
The Potomac Review	Roofline

Gratitude and Thanks

To the late Stephanie Bugen, z"l, best friend for fifty years and eagle-eyed critic, who lives on in those dear to her; she will be remembered.

To Lisa and Bill Koelewyn for time at the beach house to write.

To David James, who read this manuscript insightfully.

To the faculty and staff of the Vermont Studio Center, and of the Sewanee, Palm Beach, Key West, and Bear River writers' conferences for support and encouragement, with particular thanks to Richard Tillinghast, Keith Taylor, A. Van Jordan, Michael Dickman, Syd Lea, Jerry Dennis, Patricia Clark, Jack Ridl, Anne Marie Macari, Gerald Stern, Alan Shapiro, A. E. Stallings, Robert Hass, X. J. Kennedy, Allison Joseph, and to the late Mark Strand and Claudia Emerson, z"l, both of blessed memory.

To Jeff and Claudinne Miller, owners of the farm and B and B "Susannah's Watch" on the shores of the Patuxent River in Maryland, for their generosity and kindness during the days of final edits on this manuscript.

To Katie Lee, Acquisitions Editor at Gallaudet University Press, for guiding this collection into its current form. Her skill and diplomacy in so doing are unmatched.

About the Author

Pia Taavila-Borsheim is from Walled Lake, Michigan, and lives now in Presque Isle, Michigan, with her husband, David Borsheim, a lichenologist and bioinformation scientist.

She received her BA and MA in American Literature from Eastern Michigan University (1977, 1979) and an Interdisciplinary PhD (1985) from Michigan State University with areas of qualification in English, Sociology, and Philosophy. Before retiring in December of 2020, Taavila-Borsheim was a tenured professor of literature and creative writing in the English Department at Gallaudet University in Washington, DC.

Taavila-Borsheim's poems have appeared in journals and quarterlies including: *The Bear River Review, The Broadkill Review, Southern Humanities Review, Narrative Northeast, Tar River Poetry, Barrow Street, Threepenny Review, Wisconsin Review, Birmingham Poetry Review, Gargoyle, storySouth, The Asheville Poetry Review, 32 Poems, Measure, Ibbetson Street Review,* and *The Southern Review,* among others. She is a frequent participant at the Bear River, Sewanee, and Key West writing conferences. Her poems have been nominated for Best of the Net and Pushcart Prizes.

In 2008, Gallaudet University Press published *Moon on the Meadow: Collected Poems.* Finishing Line Press published *Two Winters* in 2011, and a chapbook, *Mother Mail,* from Hermeneutic Chaos Press, was released in 2017. *Love Poems* is out from Cherry Grove Press (2018). *Above the Birch Line* is her latest collection of poetry, Gallaudet University Press, 2021.